Questions Of Faith

Gospel Sermons For Sundays After Pentecost (Middle Third)

Cycle A

Marilyn Saure Breckenridge

CSS Publishing Company, Inc., Lima, Ohio

QUESTIONS OF FAITH

Library of Congress Cataloging-in-Publication Data

Breckenridge, Marilyn Saure, 1940-
Questions of faith : gospel sermons for Sundays after Pentecost (middle third), cycle A / Marilyn Saure Breckenridge.
p. cm.
ISBN 0-7880-1825-6 (alk. paper)
1. Pentecost season—Sermons. 2. Bible. N.T. Matthew XIII, 31-XXI, 46—Sermons. 3. Sermons, American—21st century. I. Title.
BV4300.5. .B74 2001
252'.64—dc21
2001025107
CIP

For more information about CSS Publishing Company resources, visit our website at www.csspub.com.

ISBN 0-7880-1825-6

PRINTED IN U.S.A.

These sermons are dedicated to
my grandchildren
that they may know
the love of God.

Table Of Contents

Preface

The proclamation of the Good News of Jesus Christ through the preached Word and the administration of the Sacraments has always been of primary importance in the church. Jesus Christ came preaching — "Repent, for the kingdom of heaven has come near" (Matthew 4:17). We have been called and sent out to proclaim that same Good News of the kingdom, the Good News of God's eternal reign of love.

The Matthew texts for the middle section of the Pentecost Season show us our need for Jesus Christ. Each text raises a difficult question that is ultimate for life in the kingdom. They confront us with God's law showing us our limitations, but most important, they show us God's grace that embraces us.

It is my prayer that God's law will confront us, but also that God's grace will shine through these written sermons and be a source of inspiration for those who read them.

I am grateful to the members and friends of Immanuel Lutheran Church in Wadena, Minnesota, where I am presently serving. They have supported my ministry and have responded positively to my preaching. I am also grateful to my sister Mabeth and her husband Richard, who proofread them. In addition I am most grateful to my husband Tom, who has always been my best critic and supporter.

Proper 12
Pentecost 10
Ordinary Time 17
Matthew 13:31-33, 44-52

What Is Priceless?

Introduction

What is your most priceless treasure? A friend found out the night her house was burglarized. She got up to go to the bathroom and noticed that lights were on downstairs. She thought that was strange and wondered if one of the children had come home from college unexpectedly. However as she got downstairs, she noticed that a window screen had been cut and the back door was propped open. It was then in her sleepy state that she looked to see if her piano had been taken. When she was more awake, she realized how ridiculous that was. Who would steal a piano? But it also told her what she prized most of her worldly possessions. She had worked hard to save enough money to buy that piano.

What do you prize most? Many of us work long hours in order to have a sports utility vehicle, a second home at the lake, or the best equipment with which to play golf or some other sport. And then there are others who have more money than they need and can buy anything and everything they want. That group is not just those with inherited wealth. There are young people in their twenties and thirties, not only the pro athletes and the Hollywood stars, who are entrepreneurial-minded young adults. They have done well in business and in investing and are already millionaires able to buy any toy they want. In time they will discover that even though material things can bring pleasure, they wear out and are ultimately unsatisfying.

Those who lived in the Red River Valley discovered what they prized most when they were faced with the floodwaters in 1997.

Person after person who had lost everything they owned in the flood, expressed thanks that no lives had been lost. The family was still together. They found out that it was not possessions but their families that were priceless.

That was also true of the 91-year-old widow who had spent her life accumulating worldly goods. She and her husband had worked long hours to be able to afford nice things. They had lived in a beautiful home filled with treasures. Now at age 91 she has given everything away and is living in a nursing home. She has but one thing left to give that really matters, and that is love. She tells her family frequently how much she loves them. She has learned that love — to be loved and to love — is more important than any possession.

The Kingdom Of Heaven

There is something far more priceless than possessions and even more priceless than love of family and friends. After all, our spouse, through death or divorce, will leave us. Our children will grow up and leave home. Friends will come and go. And there is a good chance that there will be times when both family and friends will disappoint us.

What then is the greatest treasure? In today's Gospel, Jesus tells us that the kingdom of heaven is the one and only thing that is priceless. There is nothing else that compares to it. It is more valuable than your business, your farm, your beautiful home, your cars, your good looks, and even your family. And the Good News is that the kingdom exists for you.

What is it and what makes the kingdom of heaven so priceless? It should be said that the "kingdom of heaven" and the "kingdom of God" are interchangeable. Matthew likely used the phrase "kingdom of heaven" because out of fear he was hesitant to write the name of God. He, like his Jewish forbears, believed that using God's name violated its holiness. In the Gospel of Mark, it is the kingdom of God that Jesus came preaching. "Kingdom of heaven" and "kingdom of God" both mean God's eternal reign of love.

In the thirteenth chapter of Matthew, Jesus tells several parables to explain the kingdom of heaven. Each parable gives us an idea of what the kingdom is like and tells us why the kingdom is priceless. What do they tell us about God's eternal reign of love?

First, the kingdom is both a present reality and a future one. We can experience it now and look forward to experiencing it in its fullness in the life to come. The kingdom of heaven will not rust out, wear out, or die. It may seem as inconspicuous and inconsequential as a mustard seed. Yet like a mustard seed and like yeast, it can bring about amazing things. The mustard seed produces the greatest shrub, and yeast can affect a whole loaf of bread. No matter how vast the world, God's reign is supreme and can transform lives.

Second, the kingdom is in the hearts of believers. A friend told me about a family she knew who had inherited wealth and were people of faith. On the surface it looked like they had everything. They owned homes in Tennessee, Colorado, and Florida. Each place was beautifully decorated and filled with antiques and original art pieces. Neither their wealth nor their faith protected them from the sorrows and pains of life. This family lost a son in an auto accident, a daughter was sexually abused by her riding instructor, one of their homes burned to the ground, and the father was recently diagnosed with cancer. They never asked, "Why us?" Instead they said, "Why not us?" Because of their faith in God, they were able to rise above these tragedies and grow from them. They kept strong and kept hope.

We can say that the kingdom of heaven is priceless in spite of suffering because the reign of God is in the hearts of believers. This means God will be with us in our suffering. In the kingdom of heaven we are transformed from fearful people to courageous people. We can have hope and peace of mind even in tragic times because as Paul writes: "We know that in everything God works for good for those who love God, who are called according to his purpose" (Romans 8:28).

Third, the kingdom is hidden joy. Even though God's reign may seem ordinary, yet when it comes, it comes unexpectedly and with joy. In fact it comes with so much joy that it is worth sacrificing everything we have for it. Jesus compares it to a treasure hidden in a field, which a laborer found and covered up, and then in his joy he sold all that he had to buy that field. And he compares it to a pearl of great value. A merchant finds it and sells everything to buy it. There is no sense of sacrifice to buy the field or the pearl. Both the laborer and the merchant will sacrifice everything to possess it because it brings joy.

Now we don't hide our treasures in fields. We are more apt to put our treasures in safety deposit boxes or in our attics or basements. We have become more aware of the value of antiques through the television show, *Antiques Road Show*. In that show, appraisers and dealers offer free appraisals on antiques and collectible memorabilia. It is both a history lesson and a treasure hunt. A painting in your attic, even if it is not a Rembrandt, may be worth thousands of dollars. An old book may be a collectors' first edition. It has been said that this show encourages people to hang on to old dishes, furniture, and other collectibles thinking that someday a piece just might be worth something and bring their children joy, even a ticket to easy street.

The kingdom of heaven is not a ticket to easy street. And it is not a joy that is dependent on externals such as wealth and worldly possessions or even on relationships. It is a joy hidden deep within us knowing that we are loved by God.

Fourth, the kingdom is costly. Both the laborer and the merchant had to sell everything to possess the treasure and the pearl. And we know the kingdom of heaven cost Jesus Christ his life. Often we forget this when we hear about God's love and that salvation is a gift to us. It is a gift to us, yet our response requires everything we have, including our lives.

Some churches have lowered the cost of discipleship to bargain basement prices. They recruit members by telling them nothing is expected of them. You may be asked to be an usher, to serve on a committee, or to sing in the choir. Then they add, come when you can. Anyone can do it. It won't take much of your time. When churches do that, they ignore an important truth: people want to find something in life that is so wonderful, so meaningful, fulfilling, and satisfying that they can give themselves to it in total commitment. People are not afraid to suffer and sacrifice, if they can find something that they think is worth it. Think of some families whose children play hockey or another sport. Once the season begins, it is all consuming. They will sacrifice everything for that sport.

The truth is that the kingdom of heaven is costly. It can cost you a lot in terms of your time and your money. There is a church in Minneapolis that has a large sculpture in the outline of the head of Christ on the front chancel wall. It is a vivid reminder to the congregation of God's love in Jesus Christ but also a reminder that members are called to be Christ's eyes, ears, mouth, hands, and feet in the world. They come to church to thank God and be nourished in order to bring the kingdom of heaven, God's eternal reign of love, into their worlds.

Finally, the kingdom is based on love. Jesus tells the parable of the net thrown into the sea to catch fish of every kind. It shows that the kingdom is for all people. It is for you no matter who you are. It is not dependent upon your economic standing, your nationality, your class, or your age. But it is dependent upon how you love.

There is a judgment time, but that judgment is different from what we might think. There is no criteria set forth for judgment in the parable. It just says that the good will be saved and the bad will be thrown out. We know from other stories in the Bible that it is a judgment not based on color of skin, blemishes, size or shape, talents, wealth, fame or education. Nor is it based on beliefs, dogmas, or creeds. It is based on love.

Those who will enter God's eternal kingdom are those who respond to the needs of others out of their love for God. Jesus will say to them:

> *"Come, you that are blessed by my Father, inherit the kingdom prepared for you from the foundation of the world; for I was hungry and you gave me food, I was thirsty and you gave me something to drink, I was a stranger and you welcomed me, I was naked and you gave me clothing, I was sick and you took care of me, I was in prison and you visited me."*
>
> — Matthew 25:34-36

Judgment time is not only a final judgment day but it is also ongoing. We experience that judgment whenever we are separated from God or our neighbors and are living only for ourselves. And likewise we experience the kingdom of heaven, God's eternal reign of love, when we are close to God and our neighbor and living for others out of our love for God. It is then when life is both challenging and exciting.

Conclusion

The kingdom of heaven is priceless. Whatever treasure you may have, the kingdom of heaven is more valuable. No matter how happy you are in your marriage, no matter if you have great health or a great career, and no matter how many places you have traveled, if you have missed out on the kingdom of heaven, you have missed out on the one thing in life whose value exceeds all others.

God's eternal reign of love here and now and forever is priceless, and it is for you and for me. It is priceless because it transforms lives giving them meaning even in suffering. It brings forth great joy that is not dependent upon external circumstances, and it is costly. It cost Jesus Christ his life. May Christ claim us that we may live in the kingdom here and now and for all eternity. Amen.

Proper 13
Pentecost 11
Ordinary Time 18
Matthew 14:13-21

How Much Is Enough?

Introduction

Is there anything better to eat than fresh homemade bread? I don't think so. I have been told that if you are trying to sell your home and are showing it, you should bake some bread so the aroma of fresh bread greets the potential buyers. You are then appealing to two senses — sight and smell. I know it would affect me positively to walk into a home that smells of homemade bread. But even better than to smell it is to eat it.

A pastor friend has a parishioner who makes the best homemade rolls. They just melt in your mouth. But there is a problem. The pastor has discovered that for her bread is not only a treat that meets her hunger needs, it is also a temptation. She hoards it and eats more than she needs or should.

I share this with you because I believe today's Gospel of the feeding of the 5,000 raises an ongoing question for all of us, whether it is bread or something else — *How Much Is Enough*? I ask this question not only in relation to bread, but to all things that we need to live. Martin Luther in his explanation of the petition, "give us this day our daily bread," in the Lord's Prayer, defines bread to include everything needed for life — "food and clothing, home and property, work and income."

How much daily bread is enough? How much bread and fish were needed for Jesus to feed the 5,000? According to today's Gospel, Jesus needed only five loaves and two fish to feed them.

The Significance Of The Miracle

This story of the feeding of 5,000 men plus women and children with five loaves and two fish is recorded in all four Gospels — Matthew, Mark, Luke, and John. This signifies to us that this was an important incident in Jesus' ministry. In fact it is the only miracle story recorded in all four Gospels.

This miracle is also depicted in early Christian art. Those who have gone on a Holy Land pilgrimage likely have seen Tabgha, a church built on the shores of the Sea of Galilee to commemorate this miracle. In the church are remnants of a magnificent mosaic floor which depicts the five loaves and two fish.

Why is this miracle so important that it is told by each of the Gospel writers and depicted in early Christian art and even has a church built to commemorate it? There were likely many reasons. For instance, perhaps each Gospel writer told it because it was the biggest church picnic ever in that day. Or perhaps they all told it to show that with God all things are possible. Or perhaps they felt this miracle story proved that Jesus truly was the Messiah, the awaited one. Or perhaps it was told to show that the way to satisfy people is to feed them. All these reasons are possibilities, but I believe it is included in all four Gospels because the multiplication of the bread and the fish shows us that God is concerned with not only the spiritual but also the physical needs of people.

The basic message of the Bible stories, including this miracle story, is God's love. God is a loving and compassionate God who came in Jesus Christ to heal, to teach, and to proclaim the kingdom of heaven, God's eternal reign of love. According to Matthew, Jesus was mourning the death of John the Baptist, his cousin and colleague who had been beheaded. Yet, when he saw the people, he forgot his need to get away and he had compassion and ministered unto them. He fed them not only spiritually but also physically with the five loaves and two fish.

The Miracle

Imagine that day when Jesus performed the miracle along the shores of the Sea of Galilee. It was getting late in the day and the crowds that followed Jesus to this place showed no sign of leaving and returning to their homes. The disciples called Jesus' attention to the potential hunger problem and encouraged him to disperse the crowd so that they could go and buy food in the villages on their way home. In those days one could not call and have pizza delivered, as we can.

Jesus had already given the people a lot of his time by teaching and healing the sick and the disciples likely thought enough was enough. Jesus disagreed and told his disciples to give the people something to eat. They thought that it was impossible. How were they to feed 5,000 men plus women and children with five loaves and two fish? How could that be enough?

It is interesting to know that in Jesus' day, bread was the mainstay of a person's diet. It was the mainstay because it could be stored and transported easily. Thus when people went on a journey, they would hide a number of loaves under their cloaks and ration it out sparingly until they were close to home. Then they would be more generous as there would be no need to bring any bread back home.

When I read this story of the feeding of the 5,000, I thought of the children's story, "Stone Soup." If you don't remember it, in one version author Marcia Brown retells an old tale of three soldiers marching down the road to a small village. The peasants see them coming and they know that soldiers are always hungry, so they hide their food under mattresses or in their barns. When the soldiers arrive and ask for something to eat, each family has a tale of woe as to why they have no food to share. The soldiers are clever and say to the people that then they must make stone soup. They begin with a kettle of water and three smooth stones. Of course if it is going to be a tasty soup, one must add some seasoning, a carrot or two, some potatoes, and some meat. Miraculously, all of these ingredients appear and they end with a soup that is fit for a king. There is more than enough for everyone. It seemed like magic.

I wonder if some of the people who were there that day to hear Jesus had bread hidden under their cloaks and did not want to share it because they were afraid they did not have enough. Only a boy, according to John's account, was willing to share what he had — five loaves and two fish.

The miracle that happened that day may have been that people began to share the bread they had hidden under their cloaks. After Jesus blessed the five loaves and the two fish and the disciples began to pass it around, perhaps the others stopped worrying about having enough and they began to take their bread from under their cloaks and began to share it. All ate and were satisfied and when the remnants were gathered, it was evident that there was more than enough. The miracle that happened that day has changed hearts. Instead of hoarding, people were willing to share.

Now some of you may be thinking that I may be trying to explain away a wonderful miracle story and not give Jesus credit for multiplying the bread and fish. I believe Jesus could do either — multiply the loaves and the fish or change hearts. Either way it was a miracle. In fact, changing hearts to share is probably harder to do than multiplying the bread and the fish. Whatever happened that day, Jesus did a miraculous thing. Five loaves and two fish were more than enough to feed the multitude.

Another Miracle Is Needed

I believe that another miracle is needed today. The question we must face is: What are we going to do about all the hungry people in the world today, people hungry for daily bread — food and clothing, home and property, work and income? According to *Bread for the World*, in the year 2000 more than 800 million people in the world went hungry. This includes twelve million children in the United States who live in households where people skip meals in order to make ends meet. There is an even greater number of people in the world living in poverty. Many are without access to basic sanitation, safe drinking water, adequate housing, health services, or nourishing food. According to the June 2000 issue of the *Ministry of Money Newsletter*, in the United States, a "developed" nation, 12.7 percent of the population fell below the official poverty level. Yet, in these last few years, there has been incredible growth in the stock market in this country. However, ninety percent of all stocks and mutual funds are owned by the richest ten percent of Americans. It seems the gap between the rich and the poor is growing wider and wider.

Now most of us are not in that ten percent group owning ninety percent of the stocks and mutual funds, but most of us have more than enough. All that is needed, according to *Bread for the World* is an estimated $13 billion a year to meet the basic health and nutrition needs of the world's poorest people, the amount that animal lovers in the United States and Europe spend on pet food in a year.

A friend told me of a family who had adopted a child who had been severely neglected. The first few weeks, even after she had plenty to eat at the table, she would wrap up food and hide it in her room. Her anxiety for food completely consumed her. In some ways many of us are like this child, especially those who have lived through tough times. It is easy to allow our fear of not having enough or our insatiable desire for material things to possess us. There is a temptation to hoard rather than share.

There is a tremendous hunger in the stomachs of many people but there is also a hunger in the hearts and souls of many people who cannot be fed by material things or by hoarding, but only by sharing.

Conclusion

The miracle of the feeding of the 5,000 shows us our role in the feeding of the hungry as disciples of Jesus Christ. In the story, the disciples were very much involved. They recognize the need — hungry people. Then they became the distributors of the food. They found out that there was more than enough when Jesus took what was available — five loaves and two fish — and blessed it. The bread and the fish became a feast for the multitude. That is what Jesus does in our lives. He takes our time and money, blesses them, and gives them back to us to use in order to show compassion to others. A miracle takes place in our hearts and as a result, God feeds millions of people with our gifts.

How much is enough? How much bread, how much money, how much compassion is needed? A lot is needed, but there is enough. God has given us more than we need or ask and just as Jesus' disciples distributed the food to the 5,000, it is through sharing that the gap between the haves and the have-nots will be narrowed.

No matter how much or how little we have, no gift is too small. After all, five loaves and two fish provided the means for a multitude to be fed. Amen.

Proper 14
Pentecost 12
Ordinary Time 19
Matthew 14:22-33

Are You A Risk Taker?

Introduction

Have you ever done anything that you thought was risky? To some degree we are all risk takers. Everything we do for the first time is a risk. For instance, some risks that most of us have taken are learning to walk, to ride a bike, to swim, to hit a ball, and to drive a car. Bigger risks which some of us have taken are getting married, having children, starting a business, inventing something, or moving across the country. These are risks because we don't know for sure what will happen. If we didn't take them, we could also be missing out on a lot of life.

Some people seem to take more risks than others and have more accidents. That seems to be true of the Kennedy family. After the plane crash that killed John F. Kennedy, Jr., newscasters raised the question of whether or not he should have taken off that night. Time and time again commentators said that the Kennedy family was famous for its appetite for risk. They did not shrink from pushing the edge of their personal abilities. And they also lived with tragedy.

Why are we willing to take risks? Usually it is because we see other people doing it and we think if they can do it, so can we. Also we are more apt to take a risk if we trust the person who is encouraging us to do it. For instance, one is more likely to do a trust fall into the arms of his/her own father than into the arms of a stranger. Risk and trust go hand and hand.

Terror At Sea

Today's Gospel is a story of terror at sea that shows both risk and trust. Peter wants to do the impossible — walk on water. He is a risk taker. Picture the scene. The disciples are sailing on the Sea of Galilee, a lake about thirteen miles long and seven and a half miles wide. Actually it is just a little larger than some of the larger Minnesota lakes. On these lakes it can be frightening when a storm hits. The wind can come up quickly and change direction so suddenly that you can get stuck out in the lake in the midst of white caps. All you can hear is the wind howling and the crashing of the waves.

In the Gospel we are told that it is evening, so I would guess that storm clouds blocked out the moon and the stars. Perhaps some lightning streaked across the sky followed by crashes of thunder. It must have been very frightening for the disciples to be in that boat being tossed about in the wind. They must have been thinking, how can this be happening to us? After all Jesus had told them to get into their boat and go to the other side, after the feeding of the 5,000, while he went up the mountain to pray. They did as they were told. Certainly you would think that they had a right to expect a nice, smooth, safe, and comfortable boat trip. Right? Wrong! Instead they were straining every muscle in an attempt to keep the boat going into the wind. Their bodies would have been tense and their faces full of fear. Likely they thought they were surely going to drown. Things were bad for the disciples and they got even worse. We learn that toward morning they saw a ghost coming toward them and they cried out in fear.

Generally speaking the disciples were not cowards, but like everyone else in the ancient world, they believed in ghosts and they were seeing a ghost. Above the noise of the storm — the crashing waves and howling wind — the disciples heard a voice. It was a familiar voice, the voice of Jesus saying, "Take heart, it is I; do not be afraid." And it is at this point that Peter cries out, "Lord, if it is you, command me to come to you on the water." And Jesus said, "Come."

Peter wanted assurance that it really was Jesus who stood on the waves before them and not a ghost. Peter took the risk of getting out of the boat and did the impossible — he started walking on the water. But when Peter noticed the strong wind and large waves, he became frightened. He began to sink. He cried out, "Lord, save me!"

A Picture Is Worth A Thousand Words

A pastor friend who studied one summer at the Ecumenical Institute in Strasbourg, France, visited a church that had a painting depicting the scene of the boat and Jesus holding onto Peter in the water. In Europe the churches are cultural centers. She said that almost every evening there would be concerts in one or two of the churches. They would go to the churches to hear the music and to see the artwork — paintings, stained glass windows, sculptures. The various art pieces in these churches taught the Bible stories. It is true that a picture is worth a thousand words.

Look around at the art you see in church. What does it teach? Most art in Christian churches shows that Jesus Christ is the one who saves. This is often simply depicted by a large cross. Or a church seeks to depict its name in art. A church by the name of Immanuel, which means God with us, has a large front piece of mosaics and stained glass that shows God with us as God the Creator depicted by stars and a logo of the world, God with us as God the Son with the manger and the cross, and God with us as the Holy Spirit by the dove in the shape of flames. It is a magnificent teaching art piece.

It was at St. Peter's Lutheran Church in Strasbourg that my friend saw the fresco depicting today's Gospel story of Peter trying to walk on water. It is a church that has had a stormy and unusual history. It was first built in the seventh century and rebuilt in the thirteenth century. In 1524 it became a Lutheran church as a result of the Reformation. In 1681 King Louis XIV gave the chancel back to the Roman Catholics, and a wall was built between the chancel and the nave. Sometime between 1895-1900 the chancel was given back to the Lutherans, and it is one of the few Lutheran churches in France today.

The painting in St. Peter's is actually a large fresco that covers the back wall of the sanctuary. A fresco is a painting done with watercolors on wet plaster. The fresco depicts the eleven disciples in the boat with Peter standing on the water holding on to Jesus. The whole story is told in that painting. The focus is on Jesus holding Peter. The message that came through to my friend from the painting was that Peter lives on the edge. The other disciples play it safe by staying in the boat. Peter in the water is the risk taker testing Jesus.

Trust And Risk

I like today's Gospel because it is a story of trust and risk. Jesus is with his disciples. It has nothing to do with the crowds of people he fed the day before and nothing to do with the Pharisees and the skeptics. It is just Jesus and his disciples. And it shows that even Jesus' disciples get into difficult situations and need reassurance at times. That would be true of us, his disciples today, we who are here in the church. There are times when we are afraid. There are times when we lose our confidence. There are times when we need to be renewed and strengthened in our faith. And that is what Jesus does for the disciples in today's Gospel. It ends with those in the boat worshiping Jesus saying, "Truly you are the Son of God."

We are here this morning in this church to worship Jesus Christ as the disciples did in the boat that day. The church has often been symbolized as a boat. In fact in many church sanctuaries, if you look up, you will see the design of an inverted ship's hull. The church, like a ship, is often in the midst of life's raging sea of problems. The church, like a ship, can be a refuge, a place that provides a respite from the storms of life. Jesus sometimes calms the storm and other times he calms us who are in the midst of the storm, giving confidence to go out to trust and risk.

In today's Gospel, Peter trusted and risked by getting out of the boat. But then he lost his trust and he began to sink. He called out to Jesus and Jesus immediately reached out his hand and caught him, saying, "You of little faith, why did you doubt?"

Is Peter doubting Jesus or himself? It seems it must be himself because he looked to Jesus to help him. It seems that Peter experienced a loss of confidence. He began to doubt himself. The lesson here may be that faith is not only placing our confidence in God to get the job done, but it is confidence that God has given us all that we need to do it. I believe trust in self is an expression of trust in God. In a way it is like the saying, "God helps those who help themselves."

I have heard some pastors say that at one time they could not believe that God had called them to proclaim God's word. Some were those who in high school could not even give a speech. Yet now they are standing in a pulpit proclaiming God's Word. To do that means they have trust that God will give them what they need to obey God's call. And when you think of those first disciples that Jesus called, it is hard to believe that God would entrust his Word to them to bring to the world. But he did and he gave them confidence that they dared risk their lives for the gospel.

Peter is perhaps the most colorful of Jesus' disciples. He is certainly the most talkative and the most eager. One moment he proclaims grandly that Jesus is the Messiah then in the next breath he tries to tell Jesus how to go about his ministry. And it is Peter who tells Jesus that even if all others forsake him, he will never forsake him. Yet three times Peter said that he never knew Jesus.

In spite of all his foibles and failings, Peter is the one who shows the most trust in Jesus. He is the risk taker. He is willing to try the impossible. I admire that because many of us are not willing to take any risks. We are afraid we will fail, or that we will look foolish, or we will do something wrong, so we do nothing. Peter, with all his imperfections, is an inspiration to us to trust and to risk.

Conclusion

The miracles which Christ performed when he was here on earth were not just walking on water or multiplying the loaves for the 5,000 or changing water into wine, but changing hearts. He changed Simon Peter from a wishy-washy being who blew in the wind to a solid rock. Christ can do that for you as well.

The Gospel for today is about Jesus Christ who is our Savior, who has not abandoned us, even in the most fearful circumstances.

It is about trust, trusting that we can risk and do what God calls us to do.

Jesus says to us, "Take heart, it is I; do not be afraid." If we keep our eyes fixed on Jesus even when the waves of life's storms are threatening, he will not let us drown. A miracle will occur, a miracle of trust — trust in God and trust in ourselves. Amen.

Proper 15
Pentecost 13
Ordinary Time 20
Matthew 15:(10-20) 21-28

Do You Have Enough Faith?

Introduction

Do you remember Elian Gonzalez who was in the news for seven months a couple of years ago? He was the six-year-old that the Cuban Americans in Miami fought to keep in the United States, a free country. His mother wanted him to be here so desperately that she died for it. Many agreed that Elian should be with his father and thus were praying until the very end that the father would seek political asylum and stay here with his family where there is freedom. But it didn't happen. Elian's father chose for them to return to Cuba, a socialist state, where there is not freedom as we know it. Over this event, many of the Cuban Americans lost faith in the United States government. And I wonder if those who prayed for Elian to stay in this country may also have lost faith in God.

Our faith is challenged when we don't get what we ask. Some people lose faith in God while others think that they didn't get what they wanted because they didn't have enough faith. The Bible is full of miraculous healing stories — lepers being cleansed, the blind regaining their sight, the crippled being able to walk, the hemorrhaging woman being healed, the daughter of Jairus, a leader in the synagogue, being healed, and as we read in today's Gospel, the story of the Canaanite woman whose demon-possessed daughter was healed. The list can go on and on. Most of these stories, including today's Gospel, imply that the person gets what he/she wants, because he or she had enough faith.

What is enough faith? Who gets it? If we don't get what we ask, does that mean we don't have enough faith?

Faith Is Bold And Persistent

The Canaanite woman in today's Gospel got what she wanted and she was both bold and persistent. She boldly intruded upon Jesus' time and even sounded rude as she kept shouting after Jesus and the disciples. The disciples encouraged Jesus to get rid of her. That may be because if Jesus talked to her, a Canaanite woman, he would be risking his reputation. After all, she was a woman and a Canaanite, and Canaanites were enemies of the Jewish people and considered to be a race that embodied all that was wicked and godless.

The woman also had to overcome her prejudices to come to Jesus because, after all, the Israelites took the Promised Land from the Canaanites. Out of love, this woman was willing to overcome any and all obstacles that stood in the way of Jesus healing her demon-possessed daughter. Now those considered demon-possessed in the New Testament were those afflicted with especially severe diseases, either physical or mental. The disease could be paralysis, loss of speech, blindness, deafness, epilepsy, or melancholy. Whatever the disease, the woman was desperate. Like most parents, she wanted the very best for her daughter.

What surprises us in this story is that Jesus was very rude to the Canaanite woman. First he rejected her by his silence. Then he said something that was cruel. He said, not directly to the woman, but to the disciples, that he was sent only to the lost sheep of the house of Israel. When he said this, Jesus was stating the common understanding of the time. The Jewish people were the chosen ones. He had come to bring the children of Israel back into the fold.

The Canaanite woman on her knees persisted, "Lord, help me!" By calling Jesus, "Lord," she addressed him as those who believed in him. Others, including opponents or cynics, called Jesus "teacher" or "Rabbi." And still Jesus had a sharp-sounding reply to her. He said: "It is not fair to take the children's food and throw it to the dogs." In other words, Jesus was asking, how can I give the blessings meant for Israel to the Gentiles? And we all know the remarkable reply of the woman, "Yes, Lord, yet even the dogs eat the crumbs that fall from their master's table." This response moved Jesus to acknowledge that this persistent, unnamed

Canaanite woman had enough faith. He sensed the depth of her response and he healed her daughter. Her boldness and persistence showed that she had enough faith.

Faith Knows No Boundaries

This story of the healing of the Canaanite woman's daughter is pivotal in Jesus' ministry. The chosen people were the Israelites, the Jews, but faith breaks down the walls. God's mercy extends to the Gentiles, as well. It is interesting to remember that within 100 years of this story, the Christian Church was made up of mostly Gentiles.

Unfortunately, we are slow to understand. Within our communities, even within the church, there are still walls between people. There are many who do not feel accepted, such as single mothers and those on the fringes of society. They stay away from church. They don't feel accepted.

Perhaps some of you know the story of Ben Hooper. As I remember it, he was born in Tennessee in the late 1800s to an unwed mother. In that era and in that community, he was called by a name that wasn't nice. His classmates made fun of him. Even at church it was not very comfortable. He and his mother would always go to church late and slip out early. One day a new preacher came to their church and he said the benediction so fast that they did not get out early enough, and they were caught in the crowd. Just about the time he got to the door, Ben felt a big hand on his shoulder and heard the preacher asking him, "Who are you? Whose boy are you?" Ben felt the old weight come upon him. It was like a big, black cloud. Even the preacher was putting him down. But as the preacher looked down at Ben, studying his face, he began to smile, a big smile of recognition. He said, "I know who you are. I see the family resemblance. You are a child of God." With that he slapped Ben on the back and told him that he had a great inheritance and that he should claim that inheritance.

Ben Hooper said that was the most significant single sentence ever spoken to him. It was a new start for him. He grew up to serve two terms from 1911 to 1915 as governor of Tennessee.

We call some people outsiders or insiders based on skin color and other conditions over which people have no control. We can't choose our parents, our nationality, our sex, or our genetic makeup, at least not yet. We may be able to do so in the future with the medical breakthrough of mapping the genome. Because of that we will be able to know who is predisposed to various diseases such as Alzheimer's, heart problems, cancer, diabetes, and epilepsy, and in time we will be able to ward them off. And in time it may also be possible to choose the genetic makeup of our children.

It is fascinating to learn that genome mapping shows that the human species traced back 7,000 generations has only a modest amount of genetic variation. The DNA of any two humans is 99.9 percent identical. The more we see that our similarities outweigh our differences, perhaps we will be able to reach out beyond our comfort zones to those whom we perceive as different from us. However, it is easier said than done.

The Evangelical Lutheran Church in America failed in meeting one of its goals. When the new church was formed in 1988, a goal was set that within ten years the membership would be ten percent people of color or whose primary language was something other than English. After ten years only 2.8 percent fit that category.

The challenge is there for us as a church. More and more new voices are being heard in our country. These new voices are challenging our established norms and values. For instance, in the next few years there will be an influx of Hmongs applying for United States citizenship. This is in response to a law Congress passed on May 26, 2000, easing the naturalization process for Hmong and Laotian veterans and their spouses. Granted most of them will stay in the larger cities where there is more work, but eventually they will migrate to the smaller communities as well.

This intrusive woman in the Gospel story reminds us that in Jesus Christ there is hope for each one of us. Not one of us has sole claim on Jesus or God. We all receive the riches of salvation as a pure gift. Sometimes that means we are healed and other times that we are not healed. That is true whether we are young or old, rich or poor, black or white, English or Spanish speaking, native American or immigrant, capitalist or socialist, industrialized or third world. Enough faith is believing that God's mercies are for you and all people.

Faith Endures God's Silence

You may be thinking, why have I not experienced God's mercy? I have been bold and persistent in my prayers. I believe that God's mercies are for all people, even me. Yet I have not gotten what I have asked of God.

Not everyone is as fortunate as the bold and persistent Canaanite woman in the Gospel. In fact I have trouble with stories like today's Gospel. Some people could interpret it to mean that if you or a loved one is not healed, it is because you don't have enough faith. I don't think this is the way it works. It is like saying God will not give you more burdens than you can bear. That sounds reassuring, but it implies that God gives us our burdens. I don't believe God piles on burdens until we reach the breaking point and then God stops. The question for us today is: Do you have enough faith to be bold and persist and keep hope even if you don't get what you want?

It is not always easy to maintain faith in God when our lives are falling apart, the world seems to be closing in on us, and God remains silent to our desperate pleas for help. More often than not we experience the silence of God such as the Psalmist who wrote: "O my God, I cry in the daytime, but you answer not." And we know that Paul, a man of great faith, prayed three times that the thorn in his flesh be removed. It wasn't. And Jesus prayed the night he was betrayed that the cup of suffering might be removed. In fact the cross is probably God's greatest silence.

We have all experienced this silence of God. We pray for something and the opposite seems to happen. For instance, we pray for sunshine for the outdoor wedding and it rains. We pray for a date to the prom and we don't get asked. We pray to get married but our significant other is not sure. We pray for reconciliation, but instead there is divorce. We pray for the right job and nothing happens. We pray for health and are plagued by some chronic illness. We pray for the life of a loved one and the loved one dies. We pray for peace in the Middle East and it doesn't happen.

The silence of God has been experienced by all of us. And this is where faith enters. It is keeping hope believing that God is with us working for our good.

Conclusion

Do you have enough faith? What do you think? Are you bold and persistent? Do you believe that God's blessings are for you even if you are an outsider? And do you keep faith even if you do not get what you ask?

Enough faith is not necessarily getting what we want but knowing that Jesus is Lord, no matter who we are and what chaos threatens us or our loved ones in life. Enough faith is to know that we are never alone. Enough faith is being patient, hoping, and not giving up no matter what. It is being confident about the future no matter how bleak the present. And it is knowing that whether we live or whether we die we belong to the Lord.

May God give each one of us enough faith. Amen.

Proper 16
Pentecost 14
Ordinary Time 21
Matthew 16:13-20

Who Is Jesus To You?

Introduction

Are you a Christian? That may seem like an inappropriate question to ask you who attend church. But you see, not everyone who attends church is a Christian. People come to church for various reasons. Many come to worship God and to be renewed for the week ahead; some come because they are facing a difficult decision and are hoping for some insights. Others come because it is the thing to do, it is a good place to make friends and business contacts, or they come to keep a spouse happy. Still others come because they want their children to learn Christian values. And if you are a young person, perhaps you come because your parents make you. By making you come, they are fulfilling the promise they made the day you were baptized. There is a good chance that we all have mixed motives for coming to worship, and that is fine. We are glad that you are here, whatever your reason, and we pray that the Holy Spirit will touch your heart this day.

The question still stands: Are you a Christian? That is a personal question that no one else can answer for you, but perhaps these questions may help.

1. Do you pray daily?
2. Do you live by the Golden Rule?
3. Do you try to keep the Ten Commandments?
4. Do you attend worship every week?
5. Do you tithe ten percent of your income?
6. Do you serve on a committee or sing in the choir?
7. Do you do volunteer work in the community?

If you said, "Yes," to most of these questions, there is a good chance that you are a Christian but not for sure. Being a good person serving others does not make you a Christian. Whether or not you are a Christian depends upon how you answer the question, "Who is Jesus to you?" This is the ultimate question because how we answer it affects not only our present life — how we spend our time and money, how we respond to others — but also how we view ourselves and our future life.

The Bottom Line

The bottom line is who is this man called Jesus who was born to an unwed mother in a stable and placed in a manger, whose earthly father was a carpenter? Who is this man who healed the sick, sought out sinners, preached the kingdom of heaven, and proclaimed Good News to the poor? Who is he?

Listen to what some of his peers said about him: "Never has anyone spoken like this!" (John 7:46). "He taught them as one having authority, and not as their scribes" (Matthew 7:29). "He has done everything well; he even makes the deaf to hear and the mute to speak" (Mark 7:37).

Yet many in Jesus' day who saw what he did and heard what he said, did not believe him to be more than a man. As we read in today's text, some thought that he was John the Baptist, who had come back to prepare the way for the Messiah, others thought he was one of the prophets who had returned — Elijah or Jeremiah. It was not unusual for people to believe that someone long dead, especially a great person, could appear again in the living flesh. In other words, the people were not sure who Jesus was, but they knew he was a great man.

There is just as much confusion today as there was in Jesus' day. Some will say he was a good man, a remarkable healer, a charismatic leader, a great teacher, a martyr, a model, a friend. He is all these things, but he must be more. Other great men are not remembered so long or have inspired so much art, music, and literature.

Nowadays it seems that people join a church more by location or by their friends or family than by their beliefs. For instance, recently a friend told me about a guest who had spent the night with her. She came late and left early the next morning, so they didn't have much time to visit. However, they talked long enough for my friend to find out the woman was a Latter Day Saint. She wanted to be sure to see the new LDS temple that had been built in Oakdale. My friend expressed surprise when she learned that the woman had become a Mormon. She thought that she was a member of the United Church of Christ as she had been when they had first met. Her guest told her that she had not only been a member of a UCC church, but also a Lutheran, and a Unitarian, and that now at age 55 she was a Mormon.

These religious bodies where she had belonged are all quite different from each other in their expectations of members and in their understanding of Jesus Christ. Yet this woman seemed comfortable in each one and now spoke enthusiastically about the Mormon religion. She was proud of the over 100 magnificent Morman temples built in the world and that the Mormons were the fastest growing church body with over ten million members. And she was proud that to belong, you are required to tithe. But when asked about what Mormons believe, she didn't really know and said she could get my friend some literature.

Now it is not so unusual for a person not to know what his/her church body believes. An article in the *Metro Lutheran* (August 2000) states that most Christians are confused about salvation. According to this article, the Mormons believe salvation is directly tied to a believer's good works in this life. Roman Catholics believe that God's grace and human behavior are both important for salvation, while Lutherans and all Protestant Christians teach that salvation is a pure gift from God, and that human behavior and good work cannot assure salvation. This understanding is based on the key argument set forth by Martin Luther in the sixteenth century that salvation is a free gift from God, and not dependent upon works. Yet a survey of 6,242 adults nationwide by The Barna Research Group showed that between fifty percent and sixty percent of Presbyterians, Lutherans, Episcopalians, and Methodists believed that a good person could earn his or her way to heaven.

Within the Christian Church there are people with many different beliefs about salvation, but whether they are Christian depends upon how they answer Jesus' question: "Who do you say that I am?" The answer to that question is more important than their theology, how they worship, and how they live their lives.

Today's Gospel is a turning point in the ministry of Jesus. It marks the end of his public ministry of traveling about from town to town, and it marks the beginning of the church. The beginning of the church is in the answer Peter gave to Jesus' question: "Who do you say that I am?" He said: "You are the Messiah, the Son of the living God." Peter got it right. It was the answer Jesus wanted to hear. God had given Peter that understanding, for Jesus says: "Flesh and blood has not revealed this to you, but my Father in heaven."

Peter's confession was an inspired and insightful declaration, and it was on this confession that Jesus is the Messiah, the Living Son of God that the church is established. On this rock, this confession, Jesus said he would build his church. This church will be so strong that nothing can prevail against it. And it is this confession that ties all Christian churches together. It is the center of the faith. It is the fulfillment of God's long-standing promise to send one who would begin the process of redeeming the world. This confession is the bottom line, the ultimate answer, or the heart of the matter. Nothing else matters because it is a declaration that Jesus Christ is the Savior and the Lord and Master of life. It is a confession that gives meaning to life. It calls forth personal commitment, loyalty, and compassion. It is a confession that inspires good works.

How Do We Come To Believe?

Each Sunday many Christian churches will confess their faith in the words of one of the creeds. When we say the Apostles' Creed, the most common of the creeds, we confess: "I believe in God, the Father almighty, creator of heaven and earth. I believe in Jesus Christ, his only Son, our Lord." How do we make that confession more than a rote reciting of the creed? How do we help people come to the understanding that Jesus is more than just a great man? How do we help people come to the place whereby they confess that Jesus is the Messiah, the one who saves and calls them to a new way of life?

As long as I can remember there have been articles in magazines and newspapers addressing the best way to educate our children in the three *R*'s and now the four *R*'s — reading, 'riting, 'rithmetic, and respect. More recently the articles have been on the state standardized tests and what should be included in them.

It is more difficult to address the question of faith development than academic development. Churches do not have standardized tests, but some churches do have expectations as to what children should memorize at each age level. But memory work is not the answer. Nor is it enough to gain mastery over the historical facts connected with Jesus of Nazareth. The goal of Christian education is not to impart knowledge but to transform lives. Thus faith is not something you can teach. It is not a skill to be learned, but a life to be experienced.

A couple of years ago a conference on Leadership in the 21st Century was held at Luther Seminary in St. Paul, Minnesota. The presenters, Bill Easum and Tom Bandy, reminded participants over and over again that we are living in a post-Christian world and we need new creative strategies to reach people for Christ. One of these new ways is through technology. In the last forty years something big has happened, and that is the web. Five hundred years ago the major event was the invention of the printing press. For the last 500 years the question was: How well can you read? But now the question is: How well can you surf the net?

We are living in what has been called the Information Age. We have access to more information than we have ever had. Computers give us information at faster and faster rates. Anything we want to know is at our fingertips with just a couple of clicks. As the church, we need to make use of this technology to inform. Still it may not be the means of transforming lives unless we use it to share our own personal faith journey.

The core issue today in this post-Christian world is how to make disciples of Jesus the Christ, the Messiah, the Son of the Living God. And we do that best by telling our own stories, why we are a Christian, and not a Buddhist or some other religion.

How many of us can tell someone why we are a Christian, and how many of us have actually done it?

Faith development may be compared to the growth of a plant. The seed is planted in the ground and then sprouts. We become aware of the new life when a blade appears above the ground. And then with water and sunlight it grows, a bud appears, and then a beautiful flower. Or if it doesn't get enough sun and water, it will shrivel up and die. This is the story of faith.

The seed is planted in baptism when we receive our identity as a child of God. The blade of faith shoots forth as a person is nurtured in the Word of God by hearing the Bible stories, singing the songs of Jesus' love, and experiencing God's love through a teacher, a pastor, or other adult. The church of Jesus Christ is a place where we are accepted and loved, where broken lives and hearts are mended, where there is forgiveness. It is here that faith is caught not taught.

The home also plays an important role in nurturing a child in the faith. Unless a parent sets the example for Christian living, there is hardly a thing the church can do for a child. There will be little growth in faith if you the parent just drop your children off at the door of the church. You the parents are the ones to whom they look. You are their role models. They need to know by your example and by your words that you believe in Jesus the Christ, the Son of the living God.

Conclusion

Faith is a gift. Paul writes in Ephesians 2:8-9: "For by grace you have been saved through faith, and this is not your own doing; it is the gift of God — not the result of works, so that no one may boast."

This gift we receive in baptism needs to be nurtured or it, like a seed that is not watered and given sunshine, will wither and die. The best way to nurture the faith is by our own lives and by our own witness to our children and those around us. Our works do not save us, but they can show that we are Christians seeking to live our life as disciples of Jesus Christ.

Perhaps you have heard the story of how Helen Keller came to learn about Jesus Christ. Helen's teacher, Ann Sullivan, invited the noted preacher, Phillips Brooks to talk to Helen. With Ann interpreting, the minister shared the gospel story. When Brooks finished, Helen Keller was beaming with pleasure. Through her teacher, Helen told the preacher that she had always known about God, but until now she didn't have a name for God.

Are you a Christian? Do you believe in Jesus Christ as your Lord and Savior? If so, there is a good chance your life will show it. Amen.

Proper 17
Pentecost 15
Ordinary Time 22
Matthew 16:21-28

What Is The Good Life?

Introduction

A while ago, a pastor friend was in Eureka Springs, Arkansas, officiating at a wedding of her nephew. Eureka Springs is like Las Vegas. You can get married with no waiting period, no blood tests, and no witnesses. Just about every motel or bed and breakfast has a sign on it that advertises "Weddings, No Waiting, Anytime."

My pastor friend asked the couple why they chose to get married in Eureka Springs since they were not eloping. They had been engaged for five months, their parents would be there for the wedding, they had witnesses, and they wanted a minister not a judge to officiate. They said they chose Eureka Springs because they wanted a romantic place and they liked its quaintness.

After the ceremony, a friend of the couple asked them why it took them so long to get married. They had known each other for six years and been living together for three of those years. The groom said he wanted to be sure she was the one to whom he wanted to commit himself for the rest of his life. The bride said that she knew he was the one she wanted to marry by their second or third date. Thus she was willing to move in with him and wait patiently — six years — until he was ready to marry her.

I share this with you because I wonder if this is not the way it is for many of us in terms of our relationship with God. God has chosen us and we are glad to receive his love, but are slow in responding, committing our lives to God. You might say we play at being a Christian, like many couples who live together play at being married. We have trouble making a total commitment. We are not sure we want to deny ourselves anything by putting someone else first in our lives.

In today's Gospel we are asked to make a total commitment, not to a spouse, but to God by denying ourselves and taking up a cross and following Jesus. This is unbelievable. It does not sound like the good life. In fact, Peter can't believe his ears when Jesus, the one he professed to be the Messiah, tells him that he, the Messiah, the Son of the living God, is to suffer and be killed. This was not Peter's understanding of the Messiah nor is it the world's understanding of a Messiah. And not only is Jesus to suffer and die, but so will his disciples. In fact, Jesus told his disciples that only those who lose their life for his sake will find it. What does it mean to lose one's life in order to find it? What is the good life and what does it take to live it?

Losing One's Life

You can have it all — intelligence, wealth, beauty, family — and yet lose your life. That was true for Ethel du Pont Warren, wife of Franklin Delano Roosevelt, Jr. Ethel had beauty, wealth, and family, yet at 49 years of age she hung herself. How sad it is when someone loses his or her life by taking it. Yet many choose this way to end a life of misery.

Suicide is an extreme way of losing one's life. There are many less dramatic ways, such as drug and alcohol abuse and becoming chemically dependent. Also there are other addictions like gambling and sex. Then, too, there are even more subtle ways of losing one's life, such as spending hours sitting in front of a screen, either a television screen — watching the soaps, talk shows, quiz shows, and sporting events or a computer screen surfing the web and visiting chat rooms or internet pornography. Technology is taking over and becoming a national obsession. In addition, there are those who lose their lives to their work, seeking success in terms of recognition and/or wealth. We all know people who have lost their spouses and their children along the way under the pressure of the drive for success in the world.

We can lose our life through suicide, various addictions, by sitting in front of a screen, and/or giving our all to be successful in the world. These are *not* the ways Jesus calls us, in today's Gospel, to lose our lives in order to save them and get the good life. For we can take and take for ourselves and even be successful in the eyes of the world, but what do we gain? Nothing! A self-serving life is empty, futile, unsatisfying, and a meaningless existence. Perhaps that kind of life can be compared to the Dead Sea. It receives fresh water, but it has no outlets. It receives and receives but never gives. Consequently nothing can live in it or around it. Instead Jesus calls us to lose our lives by giving and denying ourselves.

Denying Self

One cannot read the New Testament without realizing that Jesus expected his disciples to deny themselves. When he called his first disciples — Peter, Andrew, James, and John — he expected them to leave their boats, their families, their comfort, and their security to follow him. That was true of his other disciples as well. He called them out of relative security into radical insecurity, out of a life that was predictable into one that was unpredictable. He offered no security, no guarantee of success, no prescribed program. Like Abraham in the Old Testament, they were simply asked to leave everything to go where he called them.

As disciples of Jesus Christ, we too are called to deny ourselves. Basically denying self is dying to self, removing oneself from the center of our life and putting Christ there. It is taking our eyes off of ourselves, our trials and tribulations, our heartaches and headaches, and focusing them on Christ. It is like the discovery Copernicus, the sixteenth-century astronomer who discovered the earth is not the center of the universe, made. Rather the sun is the center and the earth revolves around the sun. When Christ is the center of our lives, things are different for us. We die to self.

In some ways that is what Christian marriage is all about — denying self and taking on the burdens of another. For Christian marriage is not just a contract where you do your share, and the other does his or her share. It is more of a covenant where you will do your part and more even when the other one does not do his/her part.

Losing one's life in order to find it means denying self not only for family and friends but also for strangers. Losing one's life to find it also includes taking up a cross.

Taking Up A Cross

Incidentally, taking up a cross is not a burden we *must* carry, but one we *choose* to carry out of our love for Christ. It is voluntary suffering for the sake of others. This is what Jesus did when he died on the cross. He said, "No one takes my life from me. I lay it down of my own accord." This is the kind of suffering Jesus is talking about in today's Gospel — "If any want to become my followers, let them deny themselves and take up their cross and follow me." Problems, tragedies in our lives, our own weaknesses are not crosses but may be consequences to our misuse of freedom or are the results of being mortal. How we choose to handle these problems may be a cross if we choose to use the situation to serve others.

Over the years there have been followers of Jesus who have chosen to take up a cross. Albert Schweitzer decided to give up his academic and social life and go to Africa. Dietrich Bonhoeffer chose to return to Nazi Germany in 1939 and share the sufferings of his people rather than teach at Union Theological Seminary in New York City.

Another example of taking up a cross would be the late Hubert and Muriel Humphrey. A retarded daughter was born to their daughter. When she was born, they first asked the question, "Why us? Why our granddaughter?" They didn't understand why. But then out of that experience came a miracle. That little girl taught them more about love than all of their life experiences. They began to understand what it means to be loved and to love. The Humphreys used the situation of their granddaughter to help other retarded children. Thus they took up a cross, the cross of making life better not only for their granddaughter but for all retarded children.

It is not only the famous who have chosen to take up a cross. People do that everyday. They choose to stay with their alcoholic or otherwise disabled spouse, or they choose out of love to leave them in order for the person to face him or herself to get the help he or she needs. I know parents who have sacrificed much for their children in order that they may go to college.

I was told that anthropologist Margaret Mead was once asked by a student, "What were some of the earliest signs of civilization in a given culture?" The student expected the answer to be a clay pot or perhaps a fishhook or a grinding stone. But Mead answered, "A healed femur." She explained that non-healed femurs are found where the law of the jungle — survival of the fittest — reigns. A healed femur shows that someone cared. Someone had to do that injured person's hunting and gathering until the leg healed. Thus compassion is the first sign of civilization.

As Christians we are prompted by our love for Jesus Christ to get involved in the lives of others. It demonstrates our faith, the belief that life is not to be hoarded but spent on others as Christ spent his life on us. A cross then is carrying something that we don't have to carry, doing something that we are under no obligation to do. But because of our faith, we do it.

Conclusion

Jesus asks, "What will it profit you if you gain the whole world but forfeit your life?" To bring that closer to home — what will it profit you if in becoming wealthy you have no time for family or friends, no time to enjoy the beauty of nature, to smell the flowers, or to look at the clouds? Or what profit is there in becoming a great scholar or scientist if you never feed the hungry, help the sick, or even be aware of the misery in the world? What gain is there in being an *A* student and having no time for volunteer work at school, at church, and in the community?

When we believe that Jesus is the Messiah, the Son of the living God, there is the danger of a cross. There is the danger that life will be upset, that it will be loaded with the burdens of others, burdens that we are not under compulsion to take up except by the compulsion of our love for Christ.

The good life happens when we totally commit ourselves to God, when we use whatever power, money, and position we have to serve others. For it is in serving others that we live the good life. We are left with the promise: "Those who lose their life for my sake will find it." Amen.

Proper 18
Pentecost 16
Ordinary Time 23
Matthew 18:15-20

Is Big Brother Watching You?

Introduction

A popular television show in 2000 was the CBS program, *Big Brother*. It was a reality-based show that allowed the viewers to watch and then vote on who should get booted out of the house. The first contestant to be expelled by the viewers was a man by the name of William, a 27-year-old youth counselor from Philadelphia. He got the boot because he had spent his first two weeks fighting with fellow housemates.

Today's Gospel deals with discipline in the church. If someone doesn't conform after being warned, they get the boot and are kicked out of church, or at least that is what it sounds like. Is that the way we should deal with sinners in the church? If we did, who would be left?

A pastor told some boys who had been making some obscene telephone calls from the church that no matter what they did, they would not get kicked out of confirmation class. Legally they might be in trouble, but the church was one place they were accepted no matter what they did. We hate the sin, but we love the sinner. Was that a good response or should they have been given the boot and kicked out of confirmation classes for a time?

Another situation that caused a great deal of debate in a church in a neighboring community was whether or not a certain woman should be allowed to teach Sunday school because she was having an affair with her boss, a married man. That same question came up in terms of a pastor. Should a pastor be allowed to continue serving a church, if he admits to having sex with one or more parishioners?

What do you think? Are there some standards or values that we must uphold as a church? And when they are ignored, are we to call each other to account? Are we our brother or sister's keeper?

Dealing With Sin

Apparently the early church had its problems with wayward members. Many of Paul's letters are written to churches to help them work through their problems. And in the Gospel reading this morning from Matthew 18, Jesus advised the church what to do in these circumstances. I believe that the advice is as good today as it was in Jesus' day.

Jesus sets forth four steps for the church to follow when there is conflict among believers due to sin. The first step was to go alone to the one who has sinned against you and tell him or her. If that doesn't bring repentance and reconciliation, go a second time with one or two witnesses. If the person still refuses to listen, a third step is to take it to the church. If these steps are done in a spirit of love, open communication, and a willingness to forgive, there is a good chance that there will be repentance and reconciliation. But if nothing happens, the fourth and last resort is excommunication from the community for the sake of the health of the church and its witness in the world.

Actually these four steps can also be used in our families. Often family feuds will go on for decades, spoiling family gatherings and never getting resolved. This happens because instead of confronting one another in love, we sit back and nurse our hurt privately. We wait for the other to apologize, and if he or she doesn't we withdraw and ignore the person. Is this happening in your family or with a friend? If so, the scripture is clear that it is the responsibility of the one who feels offended to take the first step and go to the person who has sinned against them. Often this is all it takes for a minor conflict to be resolved and families to be reunited.

A more serious sin and conflict may require that there be witnesses. Witnesses are needed so that you cannot be misquoted later.

This is particularly true in families and church families where there has been abuse. The easiest way may seem just to ignore it and get on with your life. But that doesn't happen. Both the abuser and the abused need help for healing to take place.

Not too long ago, the lead article in a local newspaper was the story of a former pastor in the community being accused of sexual misconduct while serving in a town in central Minnesota. The abused in this case, as well as all such cases, is not just the victim or victims but the whole congregation who have put their trust in that pastor or church leader. That is why church discipline sometimes requires the third step of informing the whole church in order for the church to take action. This would be true of abuse in a family, as well. The whole family needs to know, no matter how embarrassing, because the whole family is betrayed if one member abuses another. This does not mean that we force the sinner out of the home church, but that he or she is taken out of a position where he or she can do further harm.

Some Words Of Caution

It is not always easy to be our brother or sister's keeper. The process Jesus recommended for dealing with sin within the church is not as easy as it sounds. Often when there is a conflict it is not clear cut as to who is the one in the wrong. Sometimes, if not often, both have sinned. But then either one can take the first step.

The conflict in the Evangelical Lutheran Church in America over the acceptance of the historic episcopate in order to have full communion with the Episcopal Church is an example. Those against it believed that Lutherans did not need pastors ordained by bishops nor did they need bishops installed in the historic episcopate. They were afraid if it were accepted with no exceptions, the practice would one day become as essential to Lutherans as the Word and the Sacraments. This conflict, which did not necessarily have a right or wrong side, was wrong because it hurt the witness of the Christian church in the world.

As part of a church's long range planning process, there were some discussions that uncovered some minor differences of opinion. For instance, some thought members should clap after music offered by children, and others thought that we should not clap because then it becomes more of a performance than an offering to God. Another difference uncovered was concerning the exchange of God's Peace in the service. Some wanted it, and others did not want it as they felt it interrupted the flow of the service and was a way of passing germs in the cold season. Then there was the feeling expressed that the church was a social club and not an outreaching arm for Christ. Some commented that one of the church's strengths was its focus on mission, while others commented on how well the members care for each other. There was truth in all these observations.

These different perceptions people have of the church are understandable. We come from different backgrounds and have different perspectives. Many churches are made up of people who have nothing in common with each other except their love for Jesus Christ. Yet God has called us to be the church together, despite our differences. Thus we have no right to try to remove from the church those who are different from us, but it does mean we can learn from each other and work together on the essentials — a Word and Sacrament ministry that witnesses to the love of God in Jesus Christ.

Last Resort

There will always be disputes in the church because the church is made up of humans. On rare occasion there may be a time when we have to follow Christ's advice: "If the member refuses to listen even to the church, let such a one be to you as a Gentile and a tax collector." Gentiles and tax collectors were despised outsiders in Jesus' day. To treat a person as a Gentile and a tax collector, in the Jewish sense, would mean they were to be ignored. But then we need to remember that even if Jesus said that, he gave his life for sinners. He ate with sinners and even called a tax collector, Matthew, to be his disciple. Also it was Jesus who said:

> *"Whenever you stand praying, forgive, if you have anything against anyone; so that your Father in heaven may also forgive you your trespasses."*
>
> — Mark 11:25

> *"Do not judge, so that you may not be judged. For with the judgment you make you will be judged, and the measure you give will be the measure you get. Why do you see the speck in your neighbor's eye, but do not notice the log in your own eye?"* — Matthew 7:1-3

I think when Jesus says to treat someone as a Gentile or tax collector, as he does in Matthew 18, he is saying either that this must be the very last resort if all else fails or that we are to look upon the person as a Gentile or tax collector who needs to be reconverted.

As sinners we need to hear the law and the gospel so that we are both convicted of our sins and saved by Jesus Christ. If anyone is excluded from the community, how will he or she hear the Word that condemns and restores? I believe God will not allow the church to be destroyed by one or two sinners who refuse to repent and change their ways.

In the second chapter of Ephesians we are reminded that it is God who established and preserves the church and it is God who calls very diverse people together and makes a new family to be the church. Even Jews and Gentiles, who were once enemies, are no longer strangers and aliens in the church. They are members together in the household of God, built upon the foundation of the apostles and prophets, with Christ Jesus himself as the cornerstone.

Conclusion

There are expectations of us who profess to be Christians. We are expected to be moral, honest, and decent people. We are to be our brothers' and sisters' keepers. We are to look out for the weak and the voiceless. We have the responsibility to care for those not only inside of the church family but also those outside of the church and our own families.

Today's Gospel gives us good advice for dealing with each other as the church and as a family. There is a good chance that these steps will work if they are done in love and in the name of Jesus Christ. The passage ends with the much-quoted verses:

> *"If two of you agree on earth about anything you ask, it will be done for you by my Father in heaven. For where two or three are gathered in my name, I am there among them."*

Is big brother watching you? Yes, big brother, Jesus Christ our Lord and Savior, is watching you and me. He knows we are all sinners, yet he loves us and calls us to repentance. He calls us to be the church witnessing in the world for the sake of the gospel. Amen.

Proper 19
Pentecost 17
Ordinary Time 24
Matthew 18:21-35

Must I Forgive?

Introduction

As a pastor I have been asked on occasion if one must forgive another who has wronged him/her in order to receive eternal life. How would you answer that? Is the answer always, "Yes," to that question, or does it depend on the sin and the circumstance?

Are there some sins that just are not forgivable? For instance, what would you say if you were asked: "Do I have to forgive my colleague who continues to defame me to others and is ruining my reputation?" Or what would you say to the mother who tells you: "Yes, I have a son, but we don't speak to each other. I won't forgive him for stealing my retirement savings." Or what do you say to the man who still loves his wife and asks: "Should I forgive her even though she continues to be unfaithful to me?" Or what do you say to the young woman who was abused verbally, physically, or sexually by her parents? Do you tell her that she must forgive? Or how about the mother who asks you: "Do I have to forgive the drunk driver who killed my child? He has never said he was sorry."

The question is: "Must I forgive?" There is no easy answer to that question. From a quick reading of today's lessons it would seem that if we don't forgive, we are not forgiven. But I don't think it is quite so black and white.

Last Sunday's Gospel dealt with conflict in the church and the importance of going to the one who has wronged you. Today's Gospel is a continuation of that discussion. Peter asks Jesus if it is enough to forgive another member of the church seven times. He wanted to know exactly what Jesus expected of him. The rabbis of that day taught that you should forgive your brother three times. Jesus responds to Peter, "Not seven times, but, I tell you, seventy-seven times," according to the New Revised Standard Version of the Bible. In other words, there are no limits on forgiveness.

To Forgive Is Difficult

Jesus continues his teaching on forgiveness with the illustration of the unforgiving servant. The king acts mercifully, forgiving freely and unconditionally the debt of the servant. It is an incredible debt the king forgives — ten thousand talents. (A talent is worth about $1,000.) By the end of the story, the servant with the huge debt lost his forgiveness because he refused to forgive a fellow slave who owed him only a hundred denarii. (A denarii is worth about twenty cents.)

This parable of the unforgiving servant speaks directly to us today as it affirms that it is difficult for us to forgive even trivial offenses. But it also shows us there are some boundaries. The servant who would not show mercy on a fellow servant is punished. He was to be tortured until he paid his entire debt.

Some of us here know that kind of torture. We live with it day after day because we have not been able to forgive someone who has offended us, or we have not been able to forgive ourselves for something we have done that we know is wrong. A parishioner asked her pastor when God would quit punishing her for her unfaithfulness to her marriage vows. This woman believed that all the difficulties she was having in life were God's punishments. The truth was that she was punishing herself for what she thought was an unforgivable sin. In other words, not to forgive means a life of guilt and pain. Even so, it is still difficult to forgive.

There are several reasons why it is so difficult to forgive. One is that we want justice. We agree with the sayings: "As one sows, so shall one reap," or "As you make your bed, so must you lie in it." There is a truth in those sayings, but we must keep in mind that forgiveness rarely means there are no consequences of the sin. If we steal something, we may have to serve time. If we are unfaithful to our spouse, we may lose our family. If we cheat, we may get an *F* or kicked off the team. Yet, even knowing that forgiveness does not do away with the consequences of sin, it can still be difficult to forgive. It is hard to let go of feelings of anger, resentment, and even hatred because the pain is so deep. Sometimes we even want revenge.

The well-known British scholar and author, C. S. Lewis, was deeply hurt by a teacher when he was a boy. The hurt was so deep that he had difficulty forgiving, and as a Christian, this troubled Lewis. He had tried over the years again and again to forgive this schoolmaster, but it didn't work. It was not many weeks before he died that Lewis wrote a friend telling him that finally he had at last forgiven the schoolmaster who had darkened his childhood.

Many of us can identify with Lewis' feelings. It may have been a teacher or a parent, a friend or a spouse who has hurt us so deeply that we can still feel the pain. For some the pain is so intense that it is simply easier to cut that person out of our lives than to forgive. Or for some of us it is pride or embarrassment that will not allow us to forgive the person who has hurt us.

Then, too, it is more difficult for those who do not think they have done anything wrong to forgive another. But remember, to be human is to sin. There is not one of us who has not committed sins of omission. And sometimes it may be other people who encourage us to remain estranged. You may have heard someone say, "You surely are not going to forgive him after what he has done to you?" The person who says that may mean well because he or she is tired of seeing you being used and/or abused.

The hardest words we may ever say are, "I forgive you." However, it may be easier to do when we understand that forgiveness is not saying the sin never happened, or that everything is okay, or that we no longer feel the pain of the sin, because we do and we will feel the pain of it for years and years. And it does not mean that we will not remove ourselves from the situation, such as an abusive relationship. But it does mean letting go even if the other person does not ask for forgiveness and placing it in God's hands. It is you, with God's help taking the initiative, going to the person telling him/her what he/she has done that has hurt you and that you forgive. Before you can do this, you may have to ask God to give you the grace to forgive.

When Jesus says forgive seventy-seven times, it is not just for the sake of the other one but for you and me. Unwillingness to forgive hurts us more than the one who hurt us. The key verse in today's Gospel is: "Should you not have had mercy on your fellow slave, as I had mercy on you?" That is the golden rule, but even more so. Do unto others as you would have God do unto you. It is like the petition we pray in the Lord's Prayer — "Forgive us our trespasses (sin) as we forgive those who trespass (sin) against us." Are we praying, in that prayer, God to forgive us with the same love, grace, and totality that we forgive? I hope not. I do not think that is what either the petition in the Lord's Prayer or the verse from today's Gospel is saying. Rather it means we can have mercy, we are able to forgive others, when we claim God's forgiveness. If we can't forgive, it means our hearts are so filled with hate instead of love that there is no room for God's forgiveness.

To Forgive Is Healing

The goal of forgiveness is not to get over guilt but to restore a relationship with God and with our neighbor. Forgiveness is not passive resignation to a bad situation. We do not shrug our shoulders and say, "Well there's nothing else to do, I might as well forgive." There is little healing in that kind of forgiveness. Forgiveness, when it is the restoration of a relationship, is a positive, joyful activity. When we forgive we change from seeing ourselves as victims to seeing ourselves as victors. It allows us to move from weakness to strength, from inadequacy to self-affirmation. Forgiveness allows us to experience within our own lives the power and the presence of the indwelling Christ.

To be the church means we believe, as we confess in the concluding words of the Apostles' Creed, in "the communion of saints; the forgiveness of sins; the resurrection of the body; and the life everlasting." Forgiveness of sins is right up there with saints and life everlasting. Forgiveness of sins, through the death and resurrection of Jesus Christ, is the most concrete evidence of God's love for us. There is nothing more powerful than to be forgiven when you do not deserve it or expect it. And when we are able to forgive, it is a witness that we are the forgiven people of God. And when we reach out to heal brokenness through forgiveness, we are being faithful to our calling to be God's church.

One of the best modern-day examples of forgiveness that I can remember is what happened in South Africa after Nelson Mandela became president. Mandela had been imprisoned for 27 years. One would think he would come out a bitter man wanting to punish those who had taken away 27 years of his life. But it did not happen. There was no retribution, no revenge, no blood bath. Instead there was forgiveness and reconciliation.

Another example of forgiveness and reconciliation happened a few years ago when a group of 86 Lutheran youth and their advisors went on a servant event to Eastern Europe. The youth were going to build a playground for children in Poland. However, before they went to Poland, there was a home stay in Otterdorf Okrilla, a small town outside of Dresden, Germany. Now remember the Germans were our enemy during World War II. Since this part of Germany had been under communist control until the fall of the Berlin Wall in 1989, they had only limited experience with the West and Americans.

Some road construction and detours caused the busses with the youth to get lost, and the group arrived quite late. When the busses finally arrived, they were welcomed as celebrities. The streets of this little town were lined with people waving and cheering. When they arrived at the church, there were balloons, banners, and tables spread with food and drinks. After eating they all went into the church for a worship service led by their youth.

The next day the Germans went with the Americans to Dresden to be tour hosts. Dresden was a city of many art treasures. And even though it was not a military site, it was bombed by the Allies during the war. There were still signs of the bombings in the midst of restoration. In Dresden, the group gathered in a church to hear the stories of some of the survivors of the fire bombings. The survivors were all old women now and their stories were moving as they described their families and where they were when the bombs fell.

After the stories had been told, a young German man, one of the hosts, got up and asked one of the American young men to come forward with him. In broken English he said that his parents never talked about the war and he did not learn much about it in school except he knew that the United States was the enemy. The years after the war they lived under communism. Now after listening to the old women talk and the visit of the youth from the United States, he realized that he needed to ask for forgiveness from the Americans for his countrymen and women as well as the part his parents and grandparents had played in the war.

The young man from the United States, who had been asked to come forward, said, "In Jesus Christ you are forgiven." Then he went on to say, "We also ask your forgiveness for our bombing of Dresden that killed thousands and thousands of innocent people and destroyed your beautiful city. Will you forgive us?"

There was not a dry eye in that church. Can you imagine the impact that had on the youth from both countries? They heard first-hand about the destruction of war and then saw the reconciling power of forgiveness years later that is possible in Jesus Christ as the two men hugged.

When forgiveness takes place, there is healing and it brings newness of life and opens new possibilities for the future. It gives hope where there was once hurt and despair and it brings joy where there was once anger and bitterness.

Conclusion

Forgiveness is a gift from God to be passed on to others. It is not earned because if it is earned, it is not forgiveness. When we pass on the gift of forgiveness that we ourselves have received, it is the most powerful witness we have to the reality of God's grace in our own lives. It costs us nothing except to give up our pain, our bitterness, and our hate. It cost Jesus a lot — his life! This great gift is for us to receive and to give.

Must we forgive? Yes, if we want to live the new life that Christ offers now and be released from the prison of hatred, despair, and bitterness that comes when we are not able to forgive. However to forgive is not a legalistic requirement. Jesus is not trying to make a deal with us. The Good News is that Jesus forgives even our failure to forgive. He died for our sins, including our failure to forgive.

Is there someone you need to forgive in order to live the new life in Christ — an unfaithful spouse, an overbearing parent, a friend who has stabbed you in the back, an employer who has taken advantage of you? Or do you need to be forgiven for something you have done? Either way you have come to the right place. Receive the love of God in the forgiveness of your sins and then go out with the power of God's love and restore a broken relationship. Amen.

Proper 20
Pentecost 18
Ordinary Time 25
Matthew 20:1-16

Is God Fair?

Introduction

A pastor friend asked one of his parishioners, the manager of a local seed company, some questions about the seed business. He asked him, "Where do you get the seed and to whom do you sell it?" And he asked him if he needed extra laborers at certain times of the year. The manager told him that the seed company contracts with growers who raise the crops in the central area of the state in which they have a production facility. At the time they were harvesting corn. The corn was coming to them to be processed and they needed to hire some extra laborers. These extra laborers were usually migrant workers and high school students.

Then the pastor asked the manager of the seed company if he remembered the biblical story of the laborers in the vineyard where those who worked just an hour got the very same pay as the laborers who worked all day. The manager remembered the story, so the pastor asked if the seed company would ever do that — pay the extra laborers who worked only an hour the same pay as those who worked all day. Immediately the manager said: "No! If we did that, we would have a strike."

If this is the way God treats us, perhaps we should go on strike. It is outrageous. It goes against everything we have been taught. If this happened and you were one of the laborers, how would you feel if you had worked all day and received the same pay as someone who worked for only an hour? And how would you feel if you were one of the fortunate ones who had worked for only one hour and received all that money? Would it be fair? That is the question we face this morning. Is God fair?

God's Amazing Grace

What did Jesus want to teach by telling this story of the laborers in the vineyard? What is the gem of truth in it? First we need to know that the story is not about economics, how to run a business, how to increase productivity, or how to make workers happy. If the landlord had wanted to please, he would have paid each one for the job he had performed. Then there would have been no problem. What is the point of this story? I believe the point of the story is God's amazing grace. The parable shows us that God's grace is beyond our comprehension and appreciation.

Over the years, many of you who have grown up in the church have heard many interpretations of this parable. Each interpretation shows God's amazing grace. One interpretation is that God is still looking for help to work in the vineyard of the world. We may think that we are too young, or too old, or not qualified for that sort of thing. Or we may think because we are too new at being a Christian that we are not qualified. Whoever we are, God's grace is sufficient and God will give us what we need in order to work in the vineyards of our communities.

Another interpretation has been that Jesus used this story to say that everyone deserves a living wage. In Acts we read that the disciples "determined that according to their ability, each would send relief to the believers living in Judea." The message being that we need to share so that there is a more equitable distribution of wealth because God's grace, God's love, and God's blessings are intended for all people.

Still another interpretation that definitely shows God's amazing grace is that Jesus told this story to assure those who turn to Christ on their death beds that they will receive the same reward as those who have served God all their lives. In fact, a person can be immoral for most of his or her life and then repent at the last minute and receive the gift of eternal life as if he or she had always been a saint.

You may have heard versions of the story of a man who had not lived a very moral life. He was in the hospital recovering from surgery. When he regained consciousness he complained loudly to the nurse that the shades were pulled. The nurse told him to relax. A fire was burning across the street and she didn't want him to wake up and think that the operation had been a failure. We smile at this story but it depicts one view of life after death.

Whichever interpretation you prefer, the parable shows God's amazing grace. This grace comes when we least expect it or deserve it. It came to the laborers who worked for only one hour and got the same pay as those who had worked all day. It is not fair according to our way of thinking, but this should not surprise us. After all, God often seems to do the very opposite of what we expect. For example, Jesus, the Messiah of the world, came as a baby born in a stable. He came to serve rather than to be served, and he associated with tax collectors and prostitutes. He also chose what is foolish to teach the wise. And in today's Gospel he says something that is hard to accept: "The last will be first and the first will be last."

The Last Will Be First, And The First Will Be Last

It is difficult for us to comprehend that the last will be first and the first will be last. If this is the case you may be thinking: Why have I been getting up on Sunday mornings all my life to be in church? Why have I tithed? Why have I tried to lead a God-pleasing life? If you have those thoughts, let me ask you: What would you change about your life if you thought there was no eternal life with heaven or hell? Would you quit coming to church? I suspect you would change very little. If it is fear that keeps you coming to church, you probably are not getting much out of worship. Eternal life is not a reward for attending church and living the good life. Eternal life is dependent upon God's grace and not upon our own doing.

Today's parable shows us that God's grace is extravagant and that God does not think like we do. In the kingdom of heaven things are ranked, measured, and judged differently than the way we do it. It is not based on the criteria that a lemon packing plant uses in judging lemons. According to a friend who visited a lemon factory in California, it was fascinating to watch the lemons judged as they moved on a conveyer belt. After they were washed, they moved under a camera that graded them into five different categories — Sunkist, choice, standard, juice, and rejects. They were judged on the basis of size, blemishes, and color. The rejects were thrown on the field for cattle to eat. The rest were washed again, dried, waxed, and stamped. Those stamped with Sunkist were judged to be the best.

Is this the way we judge people? Do we judge them by their appearance — size, color, blemishes — plus their abilities, talents, and their wealth or lack of it? We pride ourselves on being fair and just. We value equality, and thus it upsets us when we see someone get something undeserved.

This is not the way it is in the kingdom of heaven. It is not God's way. If today's Gospel says what I think it is saying by telling us the last will be first and the first will be last, it convicts those who have been brought up in the church who think they have the only answer to salvation.

This story, like many other Bible stories, offends many of us because we see ourselves in it. Most of us identify with those who worked long hours. We think they got a raw deal, and we think we often get one too. It is so easy to feel cheated when we see someone do better, even if we get exactly what we were expecting. Fairness in our minds is determined not in terms of our commitments but in terms of what our neighbor gets. What student has not complained because another student got the same grade as she did but for half the work, irrespective of the quality? Or we become jealous when someone receives a promotion or advancement over us, maybe someone we trained for the job.

Too often our identity is based on rewards that we can compare such as grades, positions, or salaries. There is no truly fair reward system. Two farmers plant the same crop. One has a bumper harvest, the other gets nothing because worms eat up the grain. In every office there are those who do as little as possible, who take advantage of others, and then there are those who work beyond all expectations, yet both may get the same pay.

Comparing ourselves to someone else is vividly portrayed in the movie *Amadeus*. This movie dramatizes the life of Mozart. A central figure in the drama is a composer who was a contemporary of Mozart, Antonio Salieri. In the movie, Salieri is a man whose life is devoted to music. Early in his life he made a promise to God that he would give his entire life to God if God would allow him to compose music. His prayer was answered. He wrote beautiful music and was a success in his chosen vocation. He even earned a place as chief composer in the emperor's court. One day, however, he heard the music of Mozart and he realized that Mozart's musical talent was far superior to his own. Something happened within Salieri. He became obsessed with the desire to destroy Mozart. He railed against God, even though God had answered his prayer and given him great gifts. But because those gifts were not as great as Mozart's, he got mad at God. His own composing career was put on hold as he sought ways to undermine the career of Mozart. The ending to the movie is a tragic portrayal of the power of jealousy to destroy a man's heart and soul.

The movie *Amadeus* is an extreme example of jealousy, but I would guess everyone has compared him or herself unfavorably to someone else. The line that cuts to the heart in today's Gospel is when the landowner says to those who grumble, "Are you envious because I am generous?" That is a good question we need to ask ourselves when we see someone else receive God's amazing grace.

Conclusion

Today's Gospel is a story that illustrates God's judgment based on God's grace. God's judgment and grace are both amazing and exasperating. When we experience grace, it is amazing. When we see grace lavished upon others, it is exasperating and doesn't feel like grace at all. We think life is not fair, that God is not fair.

Is God fair? No, not by our way of thinking. But that is good news. We don't get what we deserve. God's goodness is not meted out on the basis of fairness, but of love. That is amazing grace. Amen.

Proper 21
Pentecost 19
Ordinary Time 26
Matthew 21:23-32

What Do You Think?

Introduction

Operation Bootstrap Africa is making a difference. It is a Minnesota based non-profit organization established in the mid-sixties to raise money to build schools in poor third world countries. The organization was founded by a pastor and his wife who served as missionaries in Tanzania for the Evangelical Lutheran Church in America (ELCA). They were determined to witness to their faith, not only with their words but also by their actions. Their commitment to make a difference by starting schools has touched the lives of many African families as well as the lives of teachers from other countries who have gone there to teach.

One teacher who went to Tanzania to teach said it was a life-changing experience for her. She found that she could live a full and satisfying life with very little in terms of material things. And she found that the Tanzanians were not a suffering people and that the missionaries and teachers who served there were not suffering people. This does not mean that they led easy lives. In fact it was more the opposite. They faced many difficulties because the people were uneducated and did not have enough water, firewood, food, or adequate health care. Yet, they were a very joyful people filled with the Spirit. You could hear and feel their joy in their singing and dancing. They lived the words in Ephesians 5:18b-20:

> *Be filled with the Spirit, as you sing psalms and hymns and spiritual songs among yourselves, singing and*

making melody to the Lord in your hearts, giving thanks to God at all times and for everything in the name of our Lord Jesus Christ.

The Tanzanians were an inspiration to the teacher from the United States. She was awed by the depth of their faith and by their joy in worshiping God. She came back saying that the church in this country needs to be reformed and that Christians needed to "walk the talk."

The teacher's observations about the church in this country have been voiced by others, as well. Some think the mainline churches have made a big mistake by not demanding more. They believe that people tend to value a religion that costs them. They value churches that demand much of their members. To these critics, the churches in this country have become soft because church members have been allowed to believe and do anything. As a result the Jesus of the scriptures — the one who fed the 5,000, who preached Good News to the poor, who drove the moneychangers out of the temple — has been reshaped to fit any passing fad. Are these criticisms of us as Christians valid? What do you think?

Walk The Talk!

In Matthew, Jesus raises that same question of the religious leaders of his day. He is in the midst of a controversy with them. They are opposing him because of his friendliness towards sinners. They can't understand why he is associating with tax collectors and prostitutes. They are trying to entrap him by asking him by what authority he does his work. Jesus answers them with a question that they refuse to answer. So he asks them: "What do you think?" and then tells them a story about a man with two sons.

In the story the father asks the sons to go into the vineyard to work. Many of Jesus' stories are set in vineyards because vineyards were important in biblical times. They provided grapes for the table and grapes for wine where clean drinking water was often scarce. Workers were urgently needed in the vineyards when the grapes became ripe.

In the story of the two sons, one son says, "I go, sir," and then does not go and the other son says, "I will not," but then reconsiders. We might say that he repents and goes into the vineyard to work. What do you think? Which son did the will of his father? The answer is obvious. Jesus was using an effective teaching technique when he asked the religious leaders what they thought. He invited them to pass judgment on this simple story, and when they did they passed judgment upon themselves. They were like the son who said, "I go, sir," but then did not go. They confessed with their lips; they said the right things but they did not act and heed the call to serve.

With which son in today's Gospel do you identify? Generally speaking, there are four kinds of people in the church: those who do not want to do anything, those who say no and then later change their minds and get involved, those who say yes to everything and then do not follow up on their commitments, and then those who do what they say. They "walk the talk."

There are many in the church who are like the son who said yes, but then didn't go into the vineyard. They are friendly, well-intentioned procrastinating people. They never argue, never criticize, or give others any problems. And yet getting them to do anything is nearly impossible. Perhaps you have heard the story of the employer who was asked to write a letter of recommendation for a rather lazy employee. The employer wanted to be honest, but he also wanted the employee to get the new job so that he would leave the company. Thus the employer concluded his letter of reference with these words: "If you get John to work for you, you will be extremely fortunate. Yours truly ..."

God is looking for followers who do more than warm a pew on Sunday mornings. God is looking for those who live the kingdom values of love and justice every day of their lives. Most of us have great intentions, and if we are honest with ourselves, we know that our words and actions don't always match. We say one thing and then do the opposite. We often procrastinate. We know the right words to say but don't always do what we say. Sometimes this happens because we want to avoid conflict or criticism at all costs. Thus we say what we know the other person wants to hear even though we have no intention of doing it. It is the easy way.

We are called not only to believe in Christ, but to follow him. To follow Christ may mean that we sometimes have to swim against the current. It is to swim up stream; it is to follow the narrow path instead of the more traveled path of the world. You may hear from your supervisor that this is the way we do it here. We have to face facts and go along with something that is against our values and principles, for the sake of the company. One who takes his/her faith seriously may respond, "Sorry, because I belong to Christ, I guess I don't belong here."

What do you think? What do you value more — words or actions? The writer of James says very clearly that faith without works is dead. The Good Samaritan was good because he saw a stranger in need and responded. The Rich Young Ruler missed out on the kingdom because he was unwilling to give his possessions to the poor. Words can be empty promises while actions show our true selves. Too often we do not "walk the talk."

Repent!

The point of this parable, however, is more than a call to action. It is a call to repent, to admit that we don't always act like the saved people we are in Jesus Christ. We do confess our faith Sunday after Sunday in church, but often we don't live it in the world. We know the Ten Commandments were given for our good, yet we don't keep them. We have other gods. We know the Bible tells us to tithe, but how many of us do? We know that we are to love and care for the poor but we don't do as much as we could. This simple story of two sons not only passes judgment upon us but it is a call to repent.

Jesus makes the point in the Gospel today that God is closer to sinners who know they are sinners than to religious people who say all the right things but do not act on their faith. This is in terms of both their personal and professional lives.

President Bill Clinton's affair with a White House intern will long be remembered. In fact it will go down in history with Clinton. At a ministers' conference of evangelicals at Willow Creek Church in Illinois, Clinton acknowledged that he made a terrible mistake, and since that mistake he has had to come to terms with many things about the fundamental importance of character and integrity. He acknowledged that he now awakens with an overwhelming sense of gratitude because he has had to come to grips with what he did. He also told the ministers that he has learned a lot about forgiveness after having to stand up and ask it for himself before the whole world. As a result, he is a far less judgmental person and far more forgiving.

It took Clinton a long time to acknowledge his sin. This was an expensive lesson for him to learn. It not only cost him a lot but also it cost the taxpayers. It did force us as a country to face questions of morality and integrity that we might not otherwise have done.

In the darkest of days, God is calling us to turn around and seek new life in him. That is what Ezekiel the prophet is saying in chapter 18 verses 30 and 31. He says: "Repent and turn from all your transgressions ... get yourself a new heart and a new spirit ... Turn then and live."

I believe that is what Jesus is telling the Pharisees, the religious leaders of his day, when he warns them that the prostitutes and tax collectors are closer to the kingdom of God than they are. He is calling them to recognize their sin and their need for him. The prostitutes and tax collectors are the ones who know it is only God who can change their heart and spirit and lift them out of a life of sin and possible death to a new life.

Today's Gospel is not as bleak as it may seem, for God challenges us with the law, showing us our limitations, but at the same time God's grace embraces us just as we are. Look around you. See the variety of people who make up God's church. Look especially at the older members, those in their nineties. You can be inspired by their lives. You know that they have gone through considerable heartache in their many decades of life. Yet they have kept the faith. And as I look out in the congregation, I see many who have "walked the talk." Some have put up with health problems for years, fighting cancer, heart disease, and other problems, but yet they have been able to give thanks and keep hope even in the darkest of days. They have a joy deep in their hearts like the Christians my friend encountered in Tanzania.

Conclusion

The story Jesus tells of the two sons invites us this morning to take stock of our lives. What do we value more — words or actions? Do we "walk the talk"? But most important, the story is a call to repentance. For if we are honest, there is truth in the criticism leveled against the Church in the United States. We could do a better job of being a voice for the disenfranchised and a safe harbor for those at sea in their lives. We could be more spirit filled, more joyful in our singing. Our actions or lack of action condemn us, but we can trust God's grace.

The well-known picture of Christ knocking on the door can be interpreted two ways — he is knocking to come in and he is knocking for us to come out into the world to live for him. I think both interpretations are correct. We need Christ in us in order to live for Christ in the world. What do you think? Amen.

Proper 22
Pentecost 20
Ordinary Time 27
Matthew 21:33-46

Why Doesn't God Do Something?

Introduction

Jesse Ventura, Governor of Minnesota, gained national media attention for his provocative comments in a *Playboy* magazine interview in 1999. In a question/answer interview, he made excuses for the Navy's Tailhook sexual harassment scandal in 1991 when 83 women were assaulted and molested at a Navy-Marine Corps gathering in Las Vegas. In addition, he thought penalties for prostitution should be lightened or else legalized. He also said that he liked to be governor most of all because it made him feel like a king and that nobody could tell him what to do.

Of all his comments in that interview, the ones he said about religion touched off the most controversy. He said, according to the October 1, 1999 *Star Tribune*: "Organized religion is a sham and a crutch for weak-minded people who need strength in numbers. It tells people to go out and stick their noses in other people's business."

Many politicians and religious leaders responded negatively to Ventura's comments on religion. One politician suggested that maybe he should consider stepping down as governor because his comments showed he had a lack of understanding for the world in which he lived. A seminary president was disappointed that the governor had no knowledge of the thoughtfulness of the many religious traditions and thought his comments showed ignorance. A United Church of Christ minister advised Ventura to stay away from churches and not to try to offer comforting words in the wake of some future tragedy.

Whether or not Ventura's comments were taken out of context, as some supporters contend, he is a self-made man who sometimes comes across as a "know it all" and someone who can take care of himself, even in a crisis.

Most of us are not as confident about ourselves as that Minnesota governor, and perhaps we are weak-minded and use our faith as a crutch. I know I wonder what people do who do not believe in God when there is a crisis. And I know others who have lost faith in God when a tragedy happens in their life or in the world. It brings to mind the age-old questions: Why does God allow suffering? Why doesn't God do something? These are certainly questions raised by today's Gospel.

Violence

Today's Gospel is another parable set in the vineyard. This one is a tragedy. It ends in violence, death, and lack of resolution. The landowner sends his slaves to the tenants to collect his produce from the vineyard. They are beaten, stoned, and killed. He sends more slaves and the same thing happens. Finally, the landowner sends his own son, and he is killed as well. We wonder what the landowner will do next. He is patient and long-suffering, both qualities we admire, yet we want him to do something to stop the killing. In fact we blame the landowner's patience and long-suffering for the death of the slaves and the son.

I don't know about you, but it makes me impatient with God. How can God allow a group of tenants to run wild in their violence? Why didn't God do something? For that matter why doesn't God do something about the violence and suffering of the innocent in our day?

You pick up any newspaper and there are examples of people suffering. I think of the eight-year-old girl who was raped by other children, one being her nine-year-old brother. I think of the innocent people killed in ethnic cleansing, including nuns and priests. I think of the random shootings on our city streets. The list can go on and on.

According to Isaiah, the vineyard is a symbol for the people of Israel, God's chosen people. Today, we believe the vineyard represents the world and we are God's chosen people who are the tenants. We have been given the responsibility to care for this world and be a blessing to all people. However, too often we not only forget to whom it belongs, we also have not done a good job of caring for the world. We have often tried to keep the vineyard for ourselves and destroyed anyone who gets in our way.

If all people of God took seriously their responsibility as tenants to care for this world, the world would be a much better place. We would not be poised on the brink of ecological disaster. Starvation would not still be a global problem. The sidewalks of major cities would not be filled with the homeless. Children would not die for the lack of food or medicine. People would not be killing each other in unthinkable numbers.

It is hard to understand, but many battles have been fought over religious beliefs. In fact, the first murder rises out of a religious act. Adam and Eve had two sons, Cain and Abel. Both sons wanted to please God, so they brought their offerings. Cain, the farmer, offers the first fruits of the soil. Abel, a shepherd, offers the first lamb from the flock. Both are generous gifts, but God plays favorites and likes Abel's gift better. Cain is so jealous he kills his brother. When asked where Abel is, Cain responds, "Am I my brother's keeper?"

Down through the ages we have witnessed sibling rivalry for God's favor. It is in the stories of Isaac and Ishmael, Jacob and Esau, Joseph and his brothers. And we see it in the conflict between Jews and Muslims, Christians and Jews, Christians and Muslims. Blood is spilled over religious convictions. In fact nearly every conflict that has occurred and is occurring on earth is driven by religious motives. Thus there was ethnic cleansing in Germany and more recently in Kosovo. Religion is also the cause for the murder of women in Afghanistan by Islamic fundamentalists seeking to keep a woman in her place. We get Muslim suicide bombers killing busloads of Jews, and a fanatical Jew mowing down thirty praying Muslims in a mosque. We get fundamental Christians killing doctors who perform abortions. Then there is Timothy McVeigh who blew up the Federal building in Oklahoma City, killing 168 people, in part as revenge against the government for killing David Koresh and his followers.

How can this be? How can those who say they love God be so violent? Or how can we, who profess we love Jesus Christ, be so self-serving? Too often we use religion to our own advantage.

Jesse Ventura, the Governor of Minnesota, said his views on religion were shaped during his military experience during the Vietnam era. He said he witnessed so-called religious leaders zealously marketing their beliefs to people too uneducated to comprehend what they were talking about and too poor to afford the money they were being asked to contribute. It is no wonder that there are those who stay away from the church or any affiliation with a religious group.

Judgment

God's word to us today is a word of judgment like the other vineyard stories. Just as surely as Jesus was judging the religious leaders of his day with the parable of the landowner and tenants, he is judging us. I am afraid the verdict is not good. We may not be violent, but we are self-serving. We don't use the resources God has given us for the good of others. We instinctively provide all that we need and more for ourselves and our loved ones and do not reach out to people who are different from us. In fact we are uncomfortable with people who are different. The worst hour at a church for a visitor is often the coffee hour after service as members gather with their friends

I will never forget the woman who confronted her pastor and her congregation. This woman, whom I'll call Debbie, called her pastor one day and said it was no use and she was calling to say good-bye. Debbie had joined this church because she wanted to have her baby baptized and she wanted him to grow up like the people in that particular church. She wanted the good life for him, not like her life. Debbie had grown up in foster families. She had been sexually abused by one of her foster fathers and his friends, raped by a person she thought she could trust, she had been on every kind of drug possible and had been apprehended for shoplifting. In order to be unattractive to men, she had become obese.

Now she had this beautiful little boy, and she wanted a different kind of life for him. But it was not working and she called to say good-bye.

Her pastor didn't understand at first, but then it dawned on her that Debbie was planning to take her own life. She asked Debbie if she and the baby wanted to come and be with her, knowing that Debbie was not very proud of her place of residency. Debbie didn't want to come. So the pastor tried to keep her talking, asking her what had happened and telling her that her baby needed her. She told her that whatever she had done, God loved her and would forgive her. But that didn't seem to work, so she said, "Debbie, I love you." Debbie's quick response was, "You are paid to love the likes of me." And that was true.

The pastor was the only one in that church who had paid any attention to Debbie and her son. The members would superficially greet her on Sunday mornings, but no one made an effort to get to know her. She and her baby needed the love and support of the members of the church and not just the pastor who Debbie said was paid to love her.

We are the tenants. We are the ones who have rejected the servants God has sent. We are the ones who killed his Son. We are the ones who are contributing to the pending ecological disaster. We are the ones who are responsible for the poor, the homeless, the dying.

It is easy to forget that we are just tenants and it is God who owns this world. It is God in whose church we are sitting this morning. All that we possess, including our homes and all that we earn, belong to God. There will be an accounting of our stewardship — the use of our time, our talents, and our resources. The gospel tells us that the kingdom will be given to "a people that produces the fruits of the kingdom."

Conclusion

There will be a day of reckoning. The picture seems dismal. Fortunately for us the landowner, God, is patient and long-suffering. We are given another chance. We can come to Christ's table and repent of our sins — sins of commission and sins of omission.

The Good News is that in Jesus Christ we are forgiven and given another chance to be faithful tenants who are a blessing to others.

When we see pain and injustice, such as an innocent child hungry and cold, don't blame God. And don't respond in anger at God when you see suffering or ask why God permits this and why God doesn't do something. The truth is that God has done something. God came in Jesus Christ to die for our sins and bring new life. And God is doing something in that God has made you and me. We can make a difference with God's help. Amen.

Lectionary Preaching After Pentecost

The following index will aid the user of this book in matching the correct Sunday with the appropriate text during Pentecost. All texts in this book are from the series for the Gospel Reading, Revised Common Lectionary. (Note that the ELCA division of Lutheranism is now following the Revised Common Lectionary.) The Lutheran designations indicate days comparable to Sundays on which Revised Common Lectionary Propers or Ordinary Time designations are used.

(Fixed dates do not pertain to Lutheran Lectionary)

Fixed Date Lectionaries *Revised Common (including ELCA) and Roman Catholic*	**Lutheran Lectionary** *Lutheran*
The Day of Pentecost	The Day of Pentecost
The Holy Trinity	The Holy Trinity
May 29-June 4 — Proper 4, Ordinary Time 9	Pentecost 2
June 5-11 — Proper 5, Ordinary Time 10	Pentecost 3
June 12-18 — Proper 6, Ordinary Time 11	Pentecost 4
June 19-25 — Proper 7, Ordinary Time 12	Pentecost 5
June 26-July 2 — Proper 8, Ordinary Time 13	Pentecost 6
July 3-9 — Proper 9, Ordinary Time 14	Pentecost 7
July 10-16 — Proper 10, Ordinary Time 15	Pentecost 8
July 17-23 — Proper 11, Ordinary Time 16	Pentecost 9
July 24-30 — Proper 12, Ordinary Time 17	Pentecost 10
July 31-Aug. 6 — Proper 13, Ordinary Time 18	Pentecost 11
Aug. 7-13 — Proper 14, Ordinary Time 19	Pentecost 12
Aug. 14-20 — Proper 15, Ordinary Time 20	Pentecost 13
Aug. 21-27 — Proper 16, Ordinary Time 21	Pentecost 14
Aug. 28-Sept. 3 — Proper 17, Ordinary Time 22	Pentecost 15
Sept. 4-10 — Proper 18, Ordinary Time 23	Pentecost 16
Sept. 11-17 — Proper 19, Ordinary Time 24	Pentecost 17
Sept. 18-24 — Proper 20, Ordinary Time 25	Pentecost 18

Sept. 25-Oct. 1 — Proper 21, Ordinary Time 26	Pentecost 19
Oct. 2-8 — Proper 22, Ordinary Time 27	Pentecost 20
Oct. 9-15 — Proper 23, Ordinary Time 28	Pentecost 21
Oct. 16-22 — Proper 24, Ordinary Time 29	Pentecost 22
Oct. 23-29 — Proper 25, Ordinary Time 30	Pentecost 23
Oct. 30-Nov. 5 — Proper 26, Ordinary Time 31	Pentecost 24
Nov. 6-12 — Proper 27, Ordinary Time 32	Pentecost 25
Nov. 13-19 — Proper 28, Ordinary Time 33	Pentecost 26 Pentecost 27
Nov. 20-26 — Christ the King	Christ the King

Reformation Day (or last Sunday in October) is October 31 (Revised Common, Lutheran)

All Saints' Day (or first Sunday in November) is November 1 (Revised Common, Lutheran, Roman Catholic)

Books In This Cycle A Series

GOSPEL SET

It's News To Me! Messages Of Hope For Those Who Haven't Heard
Sermons For Advent/Christmas/Epiphany
Linda Schiphorst McCoy

Tears Of Sadness, Tears Of Gladness
Sermons For Lent/Easter
Albert G. Butzer, III

Pentecost Fire: Preaching Community In Seasons Of Change
Sermons For Sundays After Pentecost (First Third)
Schuyler Rhodes

Questions Of Faith
Sermons For Sundays After Pentecost (Middle Third)
Marilyn Saure Breckenridge

The Home Stretch: Matthew's Vision Of Servanthood In The End-Time
Sermons For Sundays After Pentecost (Last Third)
Mary Sue Dehmlow Dreier

FIRST LESSON SET

Long Time Coming!
Sermons For Advent/Christmas/Epiphany
Stephen M. Crotts

Restoring The Future
Sermons For Lent/Easter
Robert J. Elder

Formed By A Dream
Sermons For Sundays After Pentecost (First Third)
Kristin Borsgard Wee

Living On One Day's Rations
Sermons For Sundays After Pentecost (Middle Third)
Douglas B. Bailey

Let's Get Committed
Sermons For Sundays After Pentecost (Last Third)
Derl G. Keefer

SECOND LESSON SET

Holy E-Mail
Sermons For Advent/Christmas/Epiphany
Dallas A. Brauninger

Access To High Hope
Sermons For Lent/Easter
Harry N. Huxhold

Acting On The Absurd
Sermons For Sundays After Pentecost (First Third)
Gary L. Carver

A Call To Love
Sermons For Sundays After Pentecost (Middle Third)
Tom M. Garrison

Distinctively Different
Sermons For Sundays After Pentecost (Last Third)
Gary L. Carver